The Cape and the Urn

Musings in verse on the challenge of life

Teresa Arthur

26, Forestside Crescent, Halifax, N.S., B3M 1M4 Canada

Cover Design: Aaron Arthur

Cover Photo: Dr. Sarah Nersesian

Page Design: Teresa Arthur

ISBN: 979-8-88870-527-8

Black Rose print | Public domain vectors

NOTES

The Cover Image

An explanatory note by Dr. Jeanette Boudreau
Associate Professor and Scientific Director, Beatrice Hunter Cancer Research Institute, Dalhousie University.

The use of the immune system in the fight against cancer - immunotherapy - is providing improved outcomes and better treatment options for many patients with cancer. Unfortunately, existing immunotherapies have not been highly successful in treating high grade serous carcinoma (HGSC) of the ovary.

The cover image shows a microscopic example of one HGSC tumour of the thousands being studied. The image shows a heart-shaped blood vessel, surrounded by an HGSC tumour infiltrated with different types of immune cells. This begins with the patients who generously donate their tissue to advance cancer research; to them we extend our deepest gratitude.

With research, we have learned that immune cell infiltration to HGSC tumours is associated with longer survival in patients. With research, we are trying to define new ways to recruit more immune cells into tumours, as better immunotherapies for patients with HGSC.

Like the immune system, research works best when it is done as a team. The author, Teresa Arthur has been engaged as a patient partner with the laboratory of Dr. Jeanette Boudreau, who is pursuing better immunotherapies for patients with HGSC. This photo was taken by Dr. Sarah Nersesian during her doctoral studies in the Boudreau laboratory.

Copyright

I confirm my permission to use the immunohistochemistry image of a high grade serous ovarian tumour, obtained and belonging to my laboratory, on your cover.

As you know, this image was taken in my laboratory by Dr. Sarah Nersesian, then a PhD candidate, during her doctoral research. She informs me that, she likewise, confirms her permission for you to reproduce the image on the cover.

We are grateful for your participation in our research and thrilled to support your book by providing this image for you!

AUTHOR'S NOTE

I write impulsively as and when a thought, an emotion or a feeling wakes up my Spirit. And sometimes 'wakes' is to be taken literally: It could happen in the middle of a night when I don't want to be up and scribing or in the midst of an intravenous

infusion with one arm tethered to the chemotherapy pump. So my words are raw emotion, maybe not logical or expressed in structured grammar, syntax, rhyme or rhythm. But they're my words, and I'm honoured to have birthed them and to own them.

The Spirit fountain is very dry most days now, but when I occasionally hear the tinkle of the thoughts, I give in to the urge to drink from it. To quench the inner seeking of who I'm becoming and what I'm trying to live by, always learning about my good and not so good self, my sometimes questionable principles or sometimes the niceness in my very being.

I think one should never give up on learning about who one is and the constant striving to be a better 'you' in every stage and situation. I find changes come with birth pangs from the Creator and the created: creation searching through the disorder and confusion, maybe. Finding a sliver of some clarity as to what are the 'next steps'. And accepting the person you are in the situation you're in. And I find that can bring in a Crucible-like change for me, even in tiny, minimal stages - living life fully and meaningfully as it unfolds! My Mantra. My Blessing.

Teresa

This book is dedicated to my beloved grandchildren:

Liam, Elliot, Nathaniel, Edith, Gabriel, Agnes and Evangeline.

CONTENTS

PART I

PART II

PART III

PART IV

PART V

FOREWORD

Teresa is a remarkable woman. I first met her in 1998 when she started teaching at the Sacred Heart School of Halifax (SHSH).

She was a dedicated science and religious studies teacher. Her lab was a comfortable and safe place for her students, especially over the noon hour and after school when they could get extra help, write make-up tests, share stories, get advice, or just hang out.

Teresa was a supportive colleague, always ready to offer a helping hand or a kind word. Her love of learning was evident in all her interactions, and she had the ability to find that silver lining no matter how difficult the situation.

But it was not until we had both retired from SHSH that I got to know Teresa's creative talents. We began to meet for coffee and a chat; sometimes those chats would go on for a few hours. We talked about family, life, faith, joys and sorrows.

It has been a privilege to journey with Teresa over these past eight years when she battled with cancer, but shared

with us what it is to live with it with such grace, faith, resilience and hope.

These reflections from the heart take us to Dubai, India, Goa, to the wonder of a solar eclipse, to the chemo room. They are personal moments in time when Teresa invites us in to contemplate along with her, to ponder in awe at God's creation, and to embrace our common humanity.

There is something truly mystical about Teresa's musings and reflections. I know you will find them inspirational and life giving.

Thank you, Teresa! ♡

Pauline Scott
Girls' High School Principal
Sacred Heart School of Halifax

PART I

AN UNHURRIED TIME

The unhurried glow of the first rays
Gradually waking up the rooster
The tap, tap of the toddy tapper followed
by the bicycle's horn of the baker
Doing his rounds.
An unhurried awakening of sleepy eyes
being opened
By the slow squeak of the rope, inching up
a pot of cool well-water.
The day unfurling like the pages of an
unhastily savored, favorite book.
An unhurried time that was...
The sun slowly beating down
Its fierce heat
On the green paddy fields.
A time that sowed and grew
And reaped for the people going by
With their shuffling gait.

The long, drawn-out call
Of the fisherwoman.
The silently licking flames from the
twigs that
Slowly cooked, roasted and dried,
Imparting its years of flavor
Like grandmothers cajoling, firm wisdom.
The encroaching evening rays
Mingling with the lazily drifting smoke of
dried leaves
Warming the copper kettle
Of bath water within.
The unhurried time
Never marched.
It ambled, wove its undulated etching into
An indelible memory
On and in my mind.

THE WISDOM OF CHANGE

The swinging sixties and beyond.

The times they were a-changing
The norms were old-fashioned
And the new was the thing
There was peace in the air
There was the smoke of the music
The fifties giving way to the sixties
Youth came on with valueless time
Then everything grew up.
There were decisions and traumas
And choices and no time or sense
To think things through.
You loved with your heart
And you lived with your head.
You were led by the sway
And you swam against the tide.
You pitted against the pull
And butted heads with all.
No calm, only calamities!
So you mapped your course

With no compass or stars
You had no recourse to advice
Nor plans or time to wallow
The times they then a-changed.
Amidst the dust of the desert
And the wailing of babes
And wealth being revelry of the rich??
And with the poverty of living
Came the years of famine
And the keening of the soul.
So when the oceans beyond beckoned,
And came the call of the wild
In the land of Nord
The times now are a changing again.
There is hope in the heart
But no hunger in the soul
The remnants of years stretching ahead
Towards dreams yet to dream
Reaching for the minutes and...
Even those are a-changing.

SAND AND SNOW

Memories of Dubai – of sunshine and sand dunes.

The hurrying flurries
Fall gently on the pane
Warmth from within
Melt memories -
Like the melting of dreams
Like the hurrying flurries
That dissolve into tears.
The images keep scurrying
On the mind's eye
But the here and now
Intrudes on them.
The past is fading
On the present's screen
That seems grey and dull.
Memories are visions
Of days gone by

Of sunshine on sand dunes
Like shifting memories
That speak of laughter and fun
Recapturing that time and place.

O CANADA!

The dichotomy of arrival.

Who are you? Who am I?
And then, where are you from?
You're different
You speak differently
Your food's delightful, but different.
Your accent, it's cute, but not Canadian.
You even smell, umm, umm, well you smell different.
You seem to be learning the rules
And adjusting to taxes.
But you have to go many miles

Before I can do more than just "smiles".
So, where are you from?
Well, from the same world 'out there.'
Maybe where your great-great "grampy"
sailed from.
Who sailed here and spoke differently;
Whose food was, well, delightful, but
different.
Whose cute accent was definitely not
Canadian.
Who probably smelled different
Who made all the rules
Including the one about taxes
And who would like to see
You do more than smile at the different
man.
That's because 'He became' and 'you
are' and 'I am...Canadian.'

-

ON ARRIVAL IN INDIA

The essence of time didn't change.
And neither did I.
Deeply submerged, learned reactions
bubble, and I am as before.
Years of buried behaviors
That were once the core of me
Surface like ancient shards
Brushed away by the chisel of time.
Is it memory's indelible stamp
Of long-ago living?
A certain echo of my place
in that slice of captured time?
And yet it seems out of sync
Because something has moved on,
And new patinas and newer ages
Have layered these decades
In which my older ways
Seem out of place.
Do you then justify your absence

from the people and the land,

Or just quietly forget

How it used to be

And shake off the dust

Only to bury deeper

Those old beloved memories?

Grant me the serenity

To accept this brand new face

Of an ancient land.

May I have the wisdom to

Never forget my place in time...

And move on.

WHITHER CHANGE

It still stands in my memory

The lone papaya tree

It stood stately and tall

Lanky with its tuft of broad

and flat serrated leaves

Perched atop like a ridiculous hat

In an indoor square
Of a tucked away garden.
No other flora
Keeping it company
Through the years
Of my childhood.
Every summer it withstood
The assault from my
make-shift bamboo pole
Reaching for the fruit
Almost beyond reach
Of my stubby, growing fingers.
Years, years later...
The little indoor garden
With no soil, no tree.
Bare with a concrete fill-in
The sign of the times
In this unhurried timeless land,
Goa.

AN URBAN BUMPKIN

Memories of summer village holidays

Splash!

The clay pot hits the surface of the water.

Good first try!

I peep into the well

And see my worried reflection.

Can I raise it with the rope and tackle

Without hitting the laterite well wall

And smashing it to pieces?

Smack!

The sharp coconut husk peeler tip

Connects with the coconut head.

Good aim!

I yank the handle, pierce three eyes of the nut

Can I part the tough coir

With the sharp edge

To get the tough nut loose?

Thump!

The rock flies to the ripe yellow

Mango stem

Good enough aim!

I look up to see

If the slender stock broke loose.

Did I manage to bring it down

Or was it only a shower of long slender leaves?

Whap!

The fishing line whizzes

Across the surface of the water

And plonks in.

Will the fish bite?

Was that a tug?

I reel in the line

And check the bait...

Have I got a fat wriggling fish

Or did it get away?

Whizz! Whizz!

The plump, grey cashew seed

Sizzles in the crude bonfire.

How would I know

That it can turn into

A self-propelling rocket

Fueled by its acid cover?

Did I get it out of the blaze

With the tasty nut intact?

Or was it charred to a cinder?

Lost memories with the ravages of time.

BOPPING

In April 1996, while on a ski trip to Verbier, Switzerland with friend Shahien and a group of Dubai students, we behold this wonderful sight.

Sitting on a rock head,

The stars all around us

My friend and my students

Focus on the evening sky.

The camp fire glows bright

The cold – a foreign feel while we wait

for the "sight."

Of Hale-Bopp's appeal.

The sky grows pearly grey

And soon a dark, inky blue

And then....

The star and tail appear

An awesome sight

Too good to be true!

See you - not again

In this life but

In forty three eighty five.

<u>**PART II**</u>

TO BE TWENTY

The new butterfly stretched its colour
From a cocoon newly hatched.
The new butterfly sighed.
There's so much to try.
But I'm not scared, she lied.
I am twenty, the new butterfly groaned.
I can't try enough, she moaned.
You are twenty!
The hovering mother smiles.
There's time!
You can wait awhile
To stretch your wings
To breach the reach with
Your brand new swings
My baby. Butterfly.

GRAN-MAI

I dedicated this to a cherished memory of my Gran who passed away on 14 December 2005

The chubby fingers reached out to curl
around her hand.
The hand that fed, the hand that led with
an unconditional love
For the child of the child.
Unending, forever.
Hold me grandma, feed me, love me.
Unconditionally.
The fingers reach out, to hold and lead
With ageing and gradual wrinkling skin.
The young lady reaches out
To whisper in the ear.
Secrets, plans, dreams
And her hopes she shares with the
grandmother
Who dotes as she grows.
Tell me, talk to me,

Advise me, grandma.

I always listen to you

With unconditional love

For the mother of the mother

Unending forever...

I have loved you, Granma!

WHERE WILL I GO? WHAT DO I KNOW?

The relentless ticking of the hours

Spent in deep pondering

Where will I go?

Why do I not know?

Why does my soul withhold?

I'm left here with my beliefs

Or conjectures, of faith

The last of which I hold on to...

Steadfast and strong.

Because only He lives on and has been.

And will be.

Will I become a bodyless embodiment

In Time and Space

When I have no relentless time

To be my measure.

Will I have been consumed by

endless Space

As if it was my beginning?

THE MANDOVI

The poem is dedicated to the river in Goa, India, which has always fascinated and intrigued me.

For years in time,

I've tried to gather words,

Syllables, metaphors

Like fish strung on a thin weed;

Paint a picture to emote a feeling

To express the enormity
Of this beautiful flow of liquid silver:
The Mandovi.
Watering Goa's innards to green
the land,
Squeezed from the tiny, little rivulets,
Noisy springs, gurgling brooks
Emptying into the arteries of red soil.
For years now, I've romanticized
The ebb, tides, heaving
Like a living canvas
On a firm easel.
The ballooning sails
The booming gunwales
The noisy fishing boats that plied the
Waters of the River Mandovi
Flowing from the gentle countryside,
Gathering drop after drop,
Protecting them as they churn and foam
and break onto the sloping beaches
Crashing ahead into the vast, vacant sea.

For as many years as the water has flowed
Under each bridge have I gathered
My sense of joy,
Anticipation and privilege
At being able to feel anew the emotion of belonging
Each time I feast my eyes
On this living part of me.
The Mandovi.

SHE WEEPS IN HER SLEEP

She sleeps, she weeps...
In her sleep.
Her awareness stripped away.
For her time is slipping away
Like a peel
And there are days
When she loses control
And oblivion is medicine for her soul.

What about praying?

Does she forget God?

Feels like yesterday

And myriad yesterdays

Have rolled by

When she remembered

Each and every one.

In a glorious burst of colors, faces, events

But like in a movie, it's the end. Soon.

Too soon.

Those moments of lucidity

Getting far and few

What about memories made from new?

Those are just a flash

Of a bulb on a negative film

Too much to handle.

So, she sleeps and weeps

In her sleep...singing hymns

The poem above was written for mom / Mary in 2009.

I AM

I am not a building
Concrete blocks in the earth.
These towers can fall.
I am not a tree
With roots deep in the ground
That strong winds can uproot.
I am not a person
Who can walk upon the grass
Legs can be broken.
I am not a butterfly
That hovers over the flowers
With wings that are fragile.
Am I a kite?
Loosely held in human hands
Whose breath can move me
Changing directions
As the winds blow?
Moving to the rhythm

Of my loved ones
I love to move, to drift
To soar, to dip, to adjust
To dance to the tune
Of a thousand pipers
That have held my line.
Yet I am tethered to the earth and sky
Till the kite line has done its work.
Awaiting the handing over into the arms
Of the eternal kite runner.

CHEMO ROOM INSIGHTS

Chatter of assertive reassuring voices
Interwoven with tentative, some times
feeble queries.
Even in languages other than
Your proverbial standard one.

And over all the seemingly pleasant
myriad canopy
The ever constant
Beep, beep, beep.
Of the intravenous dispensers.
Programmed by your blood
And tailored by progressive medical
research and advances
To heal what lurks in the depths
Of your broken body
But for now there's sunshine
Pouring into the fragmented spaces
Between the huge chairs
Cocooning each soul like precious silky
gossamer caterpillars ...
Waiting to emerge into
This world gone strange.
I wonder,
What ever happened sometime,
somewhere in your journey to here?

Sometimes,
I just look around at the faces.
Some stoic, others a little unsure,
Some with a tentative smile.
Preoccupied, uncommunicative or busy
with a book.
Or hands working a stitch or even
Just as I do
Trying to engage with determination,
Getting to know the dedicated angels,
familiar faces by now.
I want to know
Everyone's story
Everyone's hope
Everyone's plan
How are you coping?
Or not.
How on earth can I help you,
My unknown ships-in-the-night-friends?

LOST INSIDE

(Dedicated to those with Alzheimer's)

I wander inside...somewhere
In this vast, vague chaos.
I am worn from my hair to my
wobbly knees
And to my toes.
Do I know what I do?
Somewhere, something is broken,
Torn, shattered, nothing on cue.
Whispers in noises are spoken.
My words need to escape
From the cavern of despair
Very slowly, silkily, they drape
Into a defeated, demolished prayer.
Cracked, chipped thoughts unfold and
Transform into forgotten whimpers.
Not one thought lucidly told
Except into unfulfilled, wishful embers.

Sometimes the fogs and jumble disappear
As the mist moves, rolls to a clear day.
Then that strong me does appear
And I'm okay in a lovely kind of way.

HOPING

Soon, I'll remember things I need to say.
Stuff like: "I love you"
My brain will recollect one fine day
That I can walk.
I'm having a chat with Mister Alzheimer's.
Now, any time soon...
There'll be a cure for this deadly cancer
Early detection tests:
Then young people will not live
In such fear

That they will die soon.

I am having that talk with Ms Ovarian.

And very soon...

Heart attacks and strokes

Will be past history.

Pre-emptive methods?

Think of me solving this mystery says:

Mr. Cardiology.

I'm working on that, Mr. Heart.

Sometimes the HOPE in hopelessness

Is uselessness

It's coping with the glimmer.

Can hope be a winner?

BEING YOURSELF

He walks in the sand.

The desert man.

And imbibes the wisdom

Of the sun and the land.

No footprints he leaves because he knows

We're mere shadows

When the caravan passes.

He knows.

She tills the soil

The daughter of the land

And as she stands

Knee-deep in the paddy,

Soaks in the rain's life

Because she knows

That what we sow is

What we will reap.

She knows.

They survey the vineyard.
The family of growers
And ponder on a harvest
Dictated by heat and frost
Ancient traditions never lost
Because they know that vineyard wisdom
Is patience, hope and care?
They know.
I live in a city
An urban creature
Getting on in life
Is a daily grind of
Dependence and strife.
What do I know?
Besides consuming work
And a weekend hike?
I really don't know.

WHEN THE SUN SINKS

I wait for the sun downing
But before that my day begins.
Donning my garment
Of cheer, frantic work
Chores, more chores
Drive hither and thither
Fetch and carry
Till I yawn at mid-day.
Do lunch, feed, eat, chat
Connect with folks
And cook, eat, repeat.
I am me. But not always does
The bandwidth of my antenna
Accommodate everything, everyone.
Sometimes, the radio dial gets pushed
a bit...or a lot
And I could dissolve into static.

But mostly I await a refreshing shower.

I wind down, disconnect

And cocoon into bed

Awaiting another God-given dawn.

But that's tomorrow.

For this moment

Of lids closing on the world

Shutting out what the day brought with it.

Whatever I did with whatever it brought

All dissolving into the deep sleep of exhaustion

Or pain or forgetfulness

Just to sleep and dream.

I waited for this all day.

LONG-TERM, LONG DISTANCE

Friendships are unbroken vows
Sacred and Special
For two or for many.
Years of effort and proving oneself
And tenacity and yet
No pressure with society-imposed rules.
You were free
To go or to stay
In these unions of souls where
You grew, you grew old together,
Bonded and entwined
With these special ones
Of your own
Free will and choice.
You stayed the course,
Ran the mile, across the miles
And the joyful part?
Still sharing wisdom and smiles
Even, across the miles.

PART III

MIRROR, MIRROR

To thine own self be true.

Can always figure that out,

But how do you get it through to others?

Do you shout and say THIS IS ME?

How do you convey to all

That what they see

When you walk tall

Maybe a dwarf in giant's clothes

Masquerading as a Knight

While it is only your head that floats

And you are submerged where there is no light?

So should it be that what they saw

Is for what you stood

Or 'you' try to be, in the mirror what you see.

For who stops to better be
Stops being true.

IT'S ALL GOOD

It's all in my head.
The thoughts you may never know.
The learning that may never be said.
And with my going, may go.

It's all in my body.
The strength that compels the mind:
The pain, and the rest as well, Lordy
That I occasionally find.

It's all in my spirit
The faith that I show the world
The joy, the belief, the happiness in it
That the Lord has resolved and unfurled.

But my heart has it all...

Every event, family, person and friend

Who holds me up, lifts me when I fall

Stamped there, is clearly a loving brand.

YEAR AFTER YEAR

Year after year, I turn a new leaf

In my agenda, my life

There's always a 'thing'

Or many to scribe about.

Some drama, unexpected usually.

Some plans little or big.

Some events to anticipate.

Many plans get changed

Many events don't happen.

Many days when the 'to-do' lists

Never get done.

Some frustration, some acceptance

But there is hope

Because there is life

CARPE DIEM

It's hard to remember
When it's December
What one has done
For heaven to be won.

You look back and think
And your heart does sink
At the actions of the past
Which can't redeem you fast.

But think of them you must,
If in your future you trust.
A future of no repeat
Of the errors... now that's a feat.
Live and learn from looking back
Courage you shouldn't lack.

Be kind to talk gently...Try!
Or those resolutions go awry.

And another year wasted with no gain
All you will be left with is the pain
Of seeing the moment slip away
So carpe diem, seize each day.

MIS-COUNTING

Be cheerful (or try to be 24/7)
After all, there are 24 hours
And seven days a week
Be positive. It's not easy

There are but three hundred sixty five days
In the passage of a year
Be happy (whatever this is for you)
Every given minute remember:

Unhappiness street has a U-turn.
Be strong in adversity

Every breath lasts a nano second

You don't know your last!

Be kind to everyone

It matters what you do

Unto others,

To live with yourself.

LEARNING TO ACCEPT

Will I ever get to be ninety

Or climb a tree?

Hold a slippery fish

Or settle into a city?

Any city.

Get my spelling right

Or say what I really feel?

Will I ever pen a poem

That will ever touch your soul?

ON FALLING

I feel a sense of comfort
When my pelvis feels in sync with my toes
Right now the pain rules my mind
And comfort I cannot find.

It rules. It has rules.
The meds must have their day
Or the rest of me will pay.
But really, must it be like this?

Surely, I feel the power of this
Super Being: The Spirit within.
The grit, the determination and so....
There can be no rules. I rule.

EGOS

"UNLESS I GO, the Spirit cannot

come." (John 16:7)

Die, die to that small self

That I built into a ME

In and for all the years.

Who was I in my mother's womb?

Nascent id.

What did I do to all my inner

Bits and pieces ?

Some, I discarded,

A part, I retained,

Many, I readjusted.

Too many I might have lost..

So busy everyday

Convincing myself that I'm

This person that is best suited

To everyone else's needs

and wants and demands

And .. ah, then life for me and
all mankind in my sphere will be a win!
Who is Me? Where is Me?
Is this me?
I don't even know any more.
I know there is a BIG Spirit
Inside. Deep. Buried. Waiting.
This little 'ole I'
Has to go.
Whatever that ego.
That's when my Spirit
Will emerge.
It's on me, little one,
Leave. Go.
And then show me WHO
I really am
In Spirit.

CANCER AND CHANGE

You taught me to change.

And gave me strength when I thought

I was strong.

You got me to acknowledge who I was.

You taught me that change is not measured

by time.

But by who you see in the mirror

every time .

You made me realize that changing for the

better starts with my mind.

You made me see inside my soul

that Who created me will take me through.

The Spirit empowers me to go with the flow.

Of changes ..and how to let go.

The lessons keep changing

As the relentless challenges keep punching

But I think I've had enough .

Please Go.

YOU JUST CAN'T BE

You just can't
Take the diagnosis
And let it define
Who you were
And are going to be.
Definitely not shrink Yourself
Into an island of cancer.
Never, you just can't.
Those cells that mutated
In your core
By the trillions and more
Just did. In which ancestral line?
How? Why?
Is not now
Yours to define
And decipher and dig.
Don't let it shrink you
Into an island of cancer
No. You just shouldn't.

You carry on growing outwards
You grow inwards
Find that core of you
Where you've been
Who you always were.
Find it, if you never did before.
Now, now it's your second chance.
Can you find the strength
To change the flow
And not be that island
Of cancer.. Anymore?
A changed world
Awaits to be discovered, explored...
People to find.
New journeys into your unknown
Undiscovered self.
Who were you?
Who are you now?
Whoever you are
What you're not ....

Is this island of cancer

No. Never.

THAT FIRST STONE

The water lies still.

It is a new day, a new dawn.

The lily pad floats

The frogs spawn

And bullrushes stand tall.

But the peace

Has to be not

As I cast the first stone.

The semblance of stillness

Outside, around

But not in my soul.

How easy it is

To pick that rock or pebble

Or just lose control.

To be propelled

Into the very eye

Of the storm

That I create

With just reaching out

To break the stillness

Of the new day's dawn.

THE SHORE AND THE TRENCH

Written after a sepsis diagnosis in hospital , 2:40 a.m. Jan13, 2025

You stand at the seashore

And watch the waves

Lap your feet

Enjoy the sand between your toes.

Look at the waves.

Deal with each one that gently flows.

Enjoy each wave as it tickles your toes.

It's a cleansing when the wave recedes.

Don't look at the horizon.

Look down.

Each wave that comes to you

As an incident, an event

A lesson to be learnt.

A strategy. A plan to be worked on

To improve your life.

May be a course correction

To replan perhaps?

At an appropriate time.

This is a New Year

So many things I need to slough off

And flake away from my system,

My spirit.

And send them away with that purifying

Salty water.

Like with Julian of Norwich

It's the depths of the ocean

To where you are pulled helplessly

And where you have to just submit.
The ultimate plunging into the abyss.
But it's also about standing on the shore.
Enjoying the experience
Not just in my toes
But cajoling the feeling
Up into my soul
Where the waves lap gently,
But not always.
Sometimes there's big turbulence from
the ocean trenches
And then, will you be able to make it
Back to the shore?
Or will this tsunami
Just wash you away?
Well, it's still the age-old
Purifying, Job-like event.
Make it a practice to take the waves
Into your life. It's entropy.
Ordering, reordering, ordering again.

It's not easy.

You have to go there...to the ocean.

WAITING FOR THE BIRDS

There's no one here

But me....

I hear the fear

Of the minutes tick, tock

Into the night.

Hurried, yet slow

As they go past

The clock face

Racing into a dawn.

I wait, wait

For the birds

To herald the morn.

I'm alone. There's no one here

But me.

I hear the drip, drip

Of the rain drops.

Sometimes rhythmic

As they hit the sill.

I'm waiting, waiting

For the birds.

Yet I am not alone.

I know in my soul

That I will hear the first chirp.

Then a brief chorus.

Tentative, yet trilling

Like an orchestra

Tuning up.

And very soon

I hear, I hear the birds

And the ticking and the dripping.

And it's the dawn.

UNCERTAINTY AND INFINITY

There's the principle of the thing
Where the exclusivity of the object
Eludes the certainty of the particle
Being where you think it will be.

There's the principle of the thing
Where your finite being
Moves with the uncertainty of your life
And where you'll be at a point in time.

There's the principle of the thing
When the uncertainty of your being
Aligns with the mentality of your mind,
Convinces you that tomorrow
Might be yours to find.

There's always the Principle of the thing
Of how you eventually find your swing

Enabling the eventuality
Of your existence
To move the tick tock
Of life's clock.

So, go gently through your path
Because you know surely
That with life you will
Someday with certainty, part.

PART 1V

THE ANCIENT

It had a giant root

That kept it from falling

Through all these storms

But even a tree falls

And when it does

You can still see its strength

Amidst the gnarled roots

And twisted branches

And really ....

Did you hear it fall?

STAND STILL

Fear of losing, fear of being lost,

Fear of cowardice, fear of dying,

Fear of hurt, fear of fear itself.

Stand still.

You have to deal with it

Or admit you can't deal with it at all.
When Jesus appeared
In the upper room of Fear
He proclaimed: "Peace Be With You."
Peace. Make peace with yourself,
O warrior! Then pick yourself up
And carry on!

ECLIPSED

On 8 April 2024 ,a total solar eclipse was seen across the sky. This poem reflects that visual experience.

They were beautiful together
In a cool dude kind of way.
The sun wore the shades
And the moon donned the bling.
Shades of Selene with
Artemis on the wax
And Luna...ah, but what's in a name
It was beholding her
As Diana's avatar

Eating up Sol Invictus
As Apollo showed
His eruptions
His solar prominences.
Glorious to behold
They seemed like flames
Though not...
Just some hot air!
So male. So stale.
That dance for dominance
From Mazatlan to Maine
From Windsor to Woodstock
Was a total shadowing of the heart.
The ring of fire
The golden lining of the dark
And "Hope" the town crier.

THE TREASURES

Age is just numbers
Which whizz by in a flash.
Numbers are just digits
And pass by as years.
Precious time in minutes
Is the only treasure that lasts
On the mind's indelible eye
And makes an impact.
Treasure that you hold on to
And yet let go.
You have to.

DANCE OF THE SOUL

We meet in our souls
We dance in the rain
We're special because
We're in pain.

It's the ultimate peace
It's the eye of the storm
Though it doesn't bring calm.
It is the stillness of knowing
That I have to believe.
We draw on the unknown.
We are being moulded.
And shaped in the fire within.
We have our own glow.
Stay strong and flow
In the tempering waters
Of the cooling river
That's our mapped life.

I promise you this...

It will take you to the ocean
of riches, to the mines deep within.
Look inside yourself
To the unique treasure:

Your mountain of strength.
Work with the tools
And build your own tent!
Your weaknesses they may seem
But in truth are your pearls.
Dive deep, live in your lungs
And when you come up for air..
It will be a whole new world.
I promise you this...

SPEAKING TO THE URN

It's your turn
To speak to the urn
With no interruptions
Or arguments or back talk
Put forth in return.
You should have let
The urn have its say
When its contents

Were alive and existed as a light ,

As animated dust to love and cherish

... not now , ...not now

When it has returned to dust.

TALKING TO THE CAPE

You're worn .

Torn, patched even.

Over the years

of overuse, abuse.

Stretched to the limits of your powers.

Sometimes I wish

You didn't exist

So I wouldn't be

Super... anybody,

In all those roles.

I might have reached out, instead of

reaching out.

No regrets.

You were comfort

in the avatars you bestowed.

I learnt, I became.

My Linus- like friend.

My cape of many wonders.

SUSPENSION.

Up, up and .. where to?

The no man's airspace

That lets you float

Where you would never imagine.

Except perhaps in

An untethered air balloon

Someday, amongst

The Cappadocian fairy spires

If only your bucket

With the list hadn't

Developed that hole.

But you're up !

And the items on the list

Are more realistic

Adapted to your circumstances.

The bucket seat in the airplane

That suspends you over time

If not space

Is the next best thing

To time off.

From your body, your place

Your treatments and suspended

To-do list.

Stay up: in the air,

Spirit and soul.

Before you return to reality

Trying to be whole.

SILENT SCREAMS

Is acceptance defeat?

Or is it peace in wisdom?

I'd like it to be so.

But the flame sometimes bright

At times a-flickering

Says otherwise.

I'm sure accepting and withdrawing

Has its merits at times

But accepting that

As a way of life denies

The very meaning of life.

Is acceptance another stage in the battle?

A lull when you're gathering your forces?

A strategy, a temporary withdrawal?

A time gap, a time out

To know your strengths...

And weaknesses too.

What I won't accept is that

Acceptance is about giving up
And letting your spirit crumble and
Extinguish: a scream of the soul.

MOSAICS

When you break you don't shatter
Maybe you make a million-odd pieces
But each one matters.
Beautiful, whole you
That lies broken...
But wait.
You can be made new
If each piece is taken.
Gather, glue each piece
Into a new design.
Living as a sign of transformation
To give yourself a new lease.
As mosaic courtyards
Washed in rain and sun

Walked upon, admired, fun.
Or a Michael Angelo fresco
A creation with your shards
Or a puzzle you can be.
Learn yourself with shattered grit
Exposed but slowly fit
Into a surprising whole
With an old and new me.
Whatever you do with you
Don't lie scattered on the floor
In deafening silence
Use the howling winds of change
To set sail to a new shore.

PART V

ONE-ON-ONE: MOM AND ME

Oh mother of mine

Where did I go?

You set me adrift

At age twenty four.

That tenuous cord

So loose and broken.

I didn't feel the pull

It was just a token.

O child of mine

Why do you pull away

When you have your issues

What to me don't you say?

I'm with you in spirit

When you're not with me.

I'm your net with holes

Though through me you'll see.

MOVE ON

A floating Titanic

Sailed along

In the hope of reaching

The shore

Of promise and realized dreams.

Don't let the icy cold water of

Resentments and Unkindness

Seep in....

For the wet baggage

Will surely do you in.

O LORD OF THE UNIVERSE

Thank you Father.

The earth rotated again

And I with it.

I touched the earth

And moved and laughed

And saw the sky.

Even as my spirit flows
You kept me tethered
To down here below
Where I perhaps need to be
To grow where you plant me.
Keep the joy in me alive!
Please let me create
My happy sphere
To radiate your gift of a spirit
In need of renewal every year.

THE GARDEN AS MY TEACHER

Tomatoes, tomatoes
All in the ground
No spades, no shovels, no hoes
But they are happy in their mound.
The lessons I learn in my garden!
Optimism and patience are greater
Than you, the steward and warden of

God's earth, of which He is the Creator.
The dormant seeds lie waiting
For their food and light and water
Growing them is the breath of the Lord,
of the universe and our maker.

CONFUSED REFLECTIONS

Much unspoken, much unsaid
A lot of emotions all unexpressed
It erupts in heaving turmoil.
Was it dormant? Was it never?
Running in circles, much undone.
Too much being done, whirling agenda
No time to do, yet not really...
Time in the glass, the grains all gone?
Much to accomplish, self expectations.
Unfinished business, yet never started.

The plans, the lists, the drawing board...
Was it ever needed. Was it ever?
Choices chosen, choices regretted.
Then back to the fork, forgiveness needed.
Grace and forgiveness erupt within
Did the tide turn? Was life changed?

BEGONE EGO

From sunrise to sunset and beyond
I know I am in Your care, Lord.
Help me with joy
My burdens to bear.

Let my heart sing
As my spirit bubbles
Let me touch everything
But not be touched by troubles.

From dawn to dusk
As the hours speed
As I attempt each task,
Please, my spirit You feed.

No imagined hurts or ego
Nor I with pride be seen
But presumptions, let them go
With a heart renewed clean

DIVE DEEP

Poetry has no words.
It is a deep keening
From the soul
Asking for release.
Listen, listen with the
Ears of your heart.
It is an echo. It reverberates.
Each emotion expressed

In ever penetrating circles
Of joy, sorrow, anger
Frustration or peace.
Your soul is the endless mountain range
Capturing the thought,
Feeling the sad refrain
Like the mourner at the grave.

BOBBING ALONG

Lord, let me be that branch of a tree
A stout log that when dislodged
During a storm in turbulent surroundings
Just bobs, afloat with your mercy and
love.
It just bobs on the mad crazy waves
Gets bashed on the jutting river boulders
It just bobs along.
It bobs along.

Gets snagged by the gnarled roots
And tangled reeds
But just bobs along. Staying calm
And afloat in your promise and love
Gets lighter and detached
From the tossing of the restless
River around it
Just bobbing in faith, on the path to You.

THE WAY AND THE WALL

I live and so do you
This living of mine
Is not like yours.
Mine began years ago
When I died at birth
Or so it seemed.
Mine began
When I hit a wall
You did not

I had to decide

If I had to be

A flat Stanley Or a climber.

You didn't have to.

So I thought I could

Make my wall

A feature.

Grow climbing plants

Or paint a scape

And like Jack

Climb the stalk

Only to encounter

Not just another wall

But fee fie...a giant ...tall........

BE

The poem below was written at a Wellspring Cancer Support Foundation workshop on Resilience

Sometimes, the way to calm down

Is to be a little kite.

Leave the ground. Fly high

And be out of sight.

Find a turbulent air current

And float in super oxygen

Till you can...come back

And be yourself

(whoever you are at that moment)

And be there for them

(whoever they are at this moment)

And just be content.

Just be. Be.

SEEMINGLY SEAMLESS

"It's a beautiful quilt," they said.

Look at all the patches
The colors that blend
And patterns that meld
Into a seamless beautiful whole.
"The stitches join evenly"
They said.
Sewn with strong thread.
Well-measured, neat sashes
Amazing color splashes
That combine
Amazingly on the bed.
"But my stitches could be fake
Seemingly strong seams
Could break" said the quilt
Enjoy my glory, my comfort
Till my seamless beautiful core
Is simply no more.

THOUGHTS OF THE HEART

Can it think?

Or can it dictate

The thoughts of the head

How does it think

In a blink?

The thought is read

Into those neurons it is fed

And processed while the emotions sway.

Or is it recessed to be junked

To never see the light of day?

Thoughts in your heart that

Depart to your head

Where they are mashed into reason

And mercilessly spewed

Into well-thought-out action.

That's a faction with no traction for me.

I think with my heart alas!

COME ON, DEAR SPIRIT

The old one lives alone.
She comes for her treatment
To the hospital.
Nice, kindly nurses who speak loudly,
but gently ask questions patiently.
They describe pills with pictures.
And shapes and colours..
"Alright my dear, do you take these?"
says the perky, cheerful, optimistic 25-
something to the old one here without
support or help.
"They're house-shaped and yellow little
pills my dear."
I think the old one is hard of hearing.
Also has mobility issues
But wears a fancy pair of shoes,
And why not?
Hair coiffed, she flaunts a good
expensive handbag!

The crew leave to check out something on her chart .

The old one picks her walking cane,

her handbag, her scarf and walks away.

Tap tapping on her cane. Off home.

She doesn't want to go through the pain.

The discomfort.

Sometimes the lonely one's call

to familiar home

Is cure enough for the soul.

TRYING TO BREATHE

She struggled to write a poem..

As was her want during those

Long, endless chemotherapy sessions -

A poem about wanting to breathe.

Just to breathe.

There was nothing wrong with her lungs

Nothing wrong with the upper torso

But she just couldn't breathe.
She couldn't recall the trillion times she
must have done it, so naturally .
No struggle, no thought process.
Just dancing in the air. So what
happened ?
Just wanting to be liberated from endless
worry,
Mindless Weariness...
Care wearing her resources of energy
and air and bubbles of joy into a deflated
soda pop.
She wants the invigorating tickle of
bubbles up her nose
To feel the rush of air through her tissues
and sinews and veins.
To feel the lungs come up for gulps of air
after a good swim.
Oh, she dreams of just ..
Breathing!

TIME MOVING IN ME

Thick as molasses or runny as a brook
I'm the boatman, Or the swimmer
That sets the pace.
I'm the time traveller
And I decide if it's a race
Or just an easy float
Down the river of Time.
There's no sand in the hour glass
No shadows on the sun- dial
No rooster that proclaims dawn
But it's you that stands in the thin place
In the liminal edge of space and time.
Enter into sacred space
Tearing the veil asunder
And time follows you on your heels
But do you really have control?
You've no control on Time nor Space.
Carry on traveller
Use every minute and inch of space

That fills the time you have in seconds.
Enter back and find yourself
Move ahead and plan yourself
In this continual dance
Of the Divine in you

SHE'LL DANCE ALWAYS.

And she will live:
You will find her
In the biryanis and daals:
In the prayers for her children
In her spirit of adventure.
In the morning pancakes
In the incessant chats with friends
In her plants and in her poems...
In a heart full of love.

So what, if she'll never dance again?
So what? She has all her life...
Or what's left of it.
To try new recipes
Because cooking is her way
To love. So what if it's 'pickle
diplomacy'?
She lives in her chopping, peeling,
frying...
So what if she never cooks again?
Use her tatty notes and untidily written
diary.
So what if the sequence is wrong
And the recipes 'made up'?
As long as it conjures a flavour
A forgotten memory...
She lives... That's what!

THE ERASER

What if some day you forgot
That you were loved
By the great love of your life
Who had adored you
And had built you the Taj
And had kept his promises
To honour and cherish?
What if you forget...
His name, his face,
His caring and loving touch
His gentle kiss or his
Hungry longing gaze?
What if that love took
Wings and flew away
Out the windows of your
Memory's maze
Where all you see
Is a face, with a body

That holds you tenderly
Each day and night?
What if he cannot
Reach your soul, while you
Feel no feelings. There isn't even
confusion or a cry for help
No communication
To link that faraway
Forgotten bond of love
To your present non-being?
What will he do and feel
While he holds your hand
This stranger from a far-away
Long-forgotten land
Who does not even want
To let you go alone
To this acrid wasted place?...
Then come with me my love!

Acknowledgements

I may have turned to science for a career, but my passion for poetry - the sound and rhythm of its language - kindled when I was in primary school, never lapsed.

In recent years, now, I have been inspired by a host of poets, theologians, mystics and spiritualists and my work, in part, is influenced by their wisdom. I acknowledge all of them with gratitude. But above everything else, Holy Scripture has been my guiding light.

This book has had the moral support of a great cohort of friends. I am grateful to Dr. Jeanette Boudreau, Associate Professor and Scientific Director, Beatrice Hunter Cancer Research Institute, Dalhousie University and Dr. Sarah Nersesian, Postdoctoral Fellow - Cancer Therapeutics Program at the Ottawa Hospital Research Institute. These two wonderful academics work at the cutting edge of medical technology

and are truly amazing. Dr. Boudreau has shared some of her cancer research with me and along with Dr. Nersesian has granted me the copyright permission to use the immunohistochemistry image of a high grade serous ovarian tumour, on the cover of my book. Dr. Nersesian is the photographer of the image.

Likewise, I am in debt to Pauline Scott, the former Girls' High School Principal of the Sacred Heart School of Halifax, who graciously accepted my invitation to write the foreword to this book. Indeed, Pauline, I have cherished those coffee morning chats with you when we shared our thoughts on "family, life, faith, joys and sorrows."

I acknowledge with gratitude the kind words and the thoughts that Ivan Arthur, my dear brother-in-law, has shared in his endorsement of this book - in his own very inimitable style - to give readers an insight into what my journey with cancer has taught me.

Lastly, but not the least, I am grateful to my family, who have been my closest confidants and my everything. Thank you, Robin and Aaron. Thank you my darlings Golda and Esther and my seven grandkids - some of whom have read my poems.

Thank you Stephen Cunningham, my son-in-law, for casting your eyes on a proof copy. I am also grateful to my extended family for their moral support all these years.

www.ingramcontent.com/pod-product-compliance
Lightning Source LLC
LaVergne TN
LVHW050540100826
845148LV00002B/627

* 9 7 9 8 8 8 8 7 0 5 2 7 8 *